The Mentor

Daniel Kehlmann was born in Munich in 1975 and lives in Berlin and New York. His novels and plays have won numerous prizes, including the Candide Prize, the Doderer Prize, the Kleist Prize, the Welt Literature Prize and the Thomas Mann Prize. His novel *Measuring the World* has been translated into more than forty languages and is one of the greatest successes of post-war German literature. He is currently a fellow at the Cullman Center for Scholars and Writers of the New York Public Library.

Christopher Hampton was born in the Azores in 1946. He wrote his first play, *When Did You Last See My Mother?*, at the age of eighteen. Since then, his plays have included *The Philanthropist*, *Savages*, *Tales from Hollywood*, *Les Liaisons Dangereuses*, *White Chameleon*, *The Talking Cure* and *Appomattox*. He has translated plays by Ibsen, Molière, von Horváth, Chekhov, Florian Zeller and Yasmina Reza (including '*Art*', *Life × 3*, and *The God of Carnage*). His television work includes adaptations of *The History Man* and *Hotel du Lac*. His screenplays include *The Honorary Consul*, *The Good Father*, *Dangerous Liaisons*, *Mary Reilly*, *Total Eclipse*, *The Quiet American*, *Atonement*, *Cheri*, *A Dangerous Method*, *Carrington*, *The Secret Agent* and *Imagining Argentina*, the last three of which he also directed.

DANIEL KEHLMANN

The Mentor

translated by
CHRISTOPHER HAMPTON

FABER & FABER

First published in 2017
by Faber and Faber Limited
74–77 Great Russell Street, London WC1B 3DA

Typeset by Country Setting, Kingsdown, Kent CT14 8ES
Printed and bound by CPI Group (UK) Ltd, Croydon, CR0 4YY

A CIP record for this book is available from the British Library

ISBN 978-0-571-33964-8

FSC
www.fsc.org
MIX
Paper from
responsible sources
FSC® C013604

6 8 10 9 7 5

The Mentor, in this translation by Christopher Hampton, was commissioned by the Ustinov Studio, Theatre Royal Bath, and first presented on 6 April 2017. The cast was as follows:

Benjamin F. Murray Abraham
Martin Daniel Weyman
Gina Naomi Frederick
Erwin Jonathan Cullen

Directed by Laurence Boswell
Designed by Polly Sullivan
Lighting Designer Colin Grenfell
Composer and Sound Designer Dave Price
Casting Director Ginny Schiller CDG

Der Mentor in its original German-language production opened at the Theater in der Josefstadt, Vienna, on 8 November 2012, with Herbert Föttinger, Florian Teichtmeister, Ruth Brauer-Kvam and Siegfried Walther, directed by Herbert Föttinger.

Characters

Benjamin Rubin
a man of about seventy

Martin Wegner
early thirties

Gina Wegner
his wife, about the same age

Erwin Wangenroth
a man of about forty

THE MENTOR

Several years after the events of the play, Martin Wegner is delivering a speech.

Martin Forget him? Forget the maestro, my friend, the great Benjamin Rubin? Ladies and gentlemen, today, as I receive this prize named after him, the memories come powerfully crowding in.

> *Behind Martin, the garden of a dilapidated Art Nouveau mansion becomes visible: trees, a few garden seats, the edge of a pond, choked with reeds. Erwin Wangenroth and Benjamin Rubin step into the garden.*

We didn't need words to understand one another, precisely because, for both of us, words were our life.

Wangenroth We've been lucky with the weather, Mr Rubin. This is our garden.

Rubin Weather's overrated. At least there's somewhere to sit down.

> *He sits on one of the seats.*

Martin Is it really so many years since he left us? The history books will confirm it, but my mind refuses to accept it.

Wangenroth Did you have a good journey?

Rubin There's no such thing. There's journeys you put up with, that's all.

Wangenroth Your flight . . .?

Rubin Was two hours late. And your driver smokes.

Martin There was no constraint between us, no generation gap. There were only questions and answers, from him to me as much as from me to him.

Wangenroth You could have asked him . . .

Martin In a nutshell, from the very beginning, that was the nature of our friendship.

He looks at the two of them for a moment, then exits.

Rubin Of course I asked him not to. But the damage was done, he'd already been smoking on the way out, the car stank like hell. You shouldn't employ a driver who smokes.

Wangenroth I'm very embarrassed.

Rubin I used to smoke myself. But when the moment came to give up, I knew.

Wangenroth I'm really very . . .

Rubin Thirty years ago, if you didn't smoke, nobody took you seriously. Nowadays no one smokes, except people drinking beer and hanging around railroad stations who have no intention of getting on a train. Do you smoke?

Horrified pause.

Wangenroth No.

Rubin See what I mean! You seem a reasonable young man, Mr . . .?

Wangenroth Wangenroth. Erwin Wangenroth, ends in 'th'.

Rubin Now, about my room. I'm not demanding. But I do need more towels. A glass, a water jug. I have to take about two hundred pills a day. Mineral water,

4

please. I know the government says you can drink the stuff from the tap without a care in the world, but the government says a lot of things.

Wangenroth Of course.

Rubin Two more pillows. Not too soft. And a blanket. Not one of those hairy jobs that look as if a horse just died on it. And get rid of the rug. Rugs make me sneeze. Decades of dust. Also the TV. Are you taking notes?

Wangenroth I'll remember. What's wrong with the TV, is it not working?

Rubin Are you sure? That's what waiters always say in restaurants, I'll remember, then they have to come back and ask you again, then they still forget half of it or bring the wrong thing.

Wangenroth I'm not a waiter. What's wrong with the TV? It's brand new, it should work.

Rubin Get it out.

Wangenroth You don't want a TV?

Rubin Firstly, they give off as much radiation as a nuclear power station; and secondly, show me one thought, one poem, one worthwhile line that's ever come out of a room with a television in it.

Wangenroth Well, I . . .

Rubin See what I mean? Get rid of it! And I like a bottle of whisky on the bedside table. Cragganmore, if you can find it.

Wangenroth I'm sorry?

Rubin Craggan— Listen, Lowland malts are very safe and bland, a bit boring. Highland whiskies are bituminous, like liquid tar, like drinking smoke. Speyside malts come

5

from the border between the Highlands and the Lowlands. The Spey flows through the Eastern Highlands, then down past Balmoral, for which good Scots have never forgiven it.

He laughs. Wangenroth joins in uneasily.

But the region produces the most balanced whiskies. Cragganmore may not be the best in the world, but it's very drinkable.

Wangenroth I think we can find a bottle of Johnnie Walker.

Rubin stares at him. This answer is so wide of the mark, the only thing he can do is change the subject.

Rubin Has the young genius arrived?

Wangenroth Mr Wegner and his wife got here about an hour ago.

Rubin And this goes on for a week? Seven days?

Wangenroth Five. A working week.

Rubin I'm not an accountant. I've never worked in an office. When somebody says a week, as far as I'm concerned, that means seven days.

Wangenroth You're welcome to stay seven days.

Rubin Oh God, no! Is this whole thing your idea?

Wangenroth It's an initiative of our Foundation. At the moment cultural sponsorship is very much in favour of mentoring projects.

Rubin 'Mentoring projects'?

Wangenroth Don't you like the idea?

Rubin I don't like the expression. The idea I like, since it's paying me so well.

Wangenroth I can't imagine someone like Benjamin Rubin would agree to this simply for the money.

Rubin Feel free to imagine it. He's here with his wife?

Wangenroth An art historian.

Rubin Interesting. In my day, women who studied art were . . . That's very interesting.

Wangenroth Mr Rubin, please allow me to take advantage of this moment together and tell you how much your work means to me.

Rubin Ah.

Wangenroth I was still at school when I read your play, and . . .

Rubin Which play?

Wangenroth Well, *The Long Road*, obviously.

Rubin I have written other plays. Nine other plays. As well as two novels and twelve screenplays.

Wangenroth Of course, but *The Long Road* was . . .

Rubin I know what you mean.

Wangenroth In any case, for me *The Long Road* was . . .

Rubin When people tell me I've never written another play like it, my answer is, maybe so, but neither has anyone else.

Wangenroth laughs. Then he fetches out a paperback and a ballpoint pen.

Wangenroth Could you perhaps . . . ?

Rubin Hand it over. I've done this so often, it's the unsigned ones that are the rare ones. Much sought after. How do you spell Wangenroth?

Wangenroth If you could inscribe it 'For Erwin'. I'd prefer that.

Rubin 'Th' at the end?

Wangenroth takes a moment to grasp his meaning.

Wangenroth Yes. Wangenroth.

Rubin is signing the copy. Martin and Gina Wegner arrive. Rubin doesn't notice them.

Martin Mr Rubin?

Rubin seems absorbed in his signing.

Dr Livingstone, I presume?

Rubin closes the book and hands it back to Wangenroth. Only then, after an almost provocative pause, does he turn to Martin.

Rubin What?

Martin Just a joke.

Rubin Livingstone?

Martin When Henry Morton Stanley, the renowned explorer, after years of searching through the jungle, encountered the long-vanished Livingstone, he said . . . Just a joke. Doesn't matter.

Rubin He said 'just a joke'?

Martin He said, 'Dr Livingstone, I presume.'

Pause.

Rubin So?

Martin A joke. Wasn't really thinking. Nice to meet you.

He extends a hand towards Rubin, who accepts it cautiously.

Rubin I've heard a lot about you.

Martin I find that difficult to believe.

Rubin And you . . . ?

Gina Gina.

Rubin takes her extended hand and kisses it.

I first read *The Long Road* when I was at school.

Rubin Not so long ago, by the looks of you.

Gina Then I read it twice more. I'd so love to see a production of it.

Rubin It hasn't been revived for a long time.

Gina You were only twenty-four. How could you write something like that?

Rubin Sometimes I'm asked why I never wrote another play like it. I always say: 'Who has?'

Gina and Martin laugh. Wangenroth, already familiar with the joke, does not.

So how's it going to work? We have to faff about with your play for five days?

Martin It's my first time at this as well.

Rubin I'm being paid, I'm all yours. If an old fossil can be any use at all to the voice of his generation.

Martin Did you read that somewhere?

Rubin I never read newspapers. But Mr Wangenroth sent me copies of your reviews. 'The voice of his generation'. Not bad.

Martin Unfortunately it was only in the online edition, in August, what's more. Everyone was on holiday. Although it does pop up if you google me.

Rubin How much are they paying you?

Martin Here? Ten thousand.

Rubin Seriously?

Martin Perhaps I shouldn't have said . . . Yes, I'm getting ten thousand.

Rubin You're paying him ten thousand? Really?

Wangenroth You're both getting the same fee, ten thousand euros. Obviously.

Martin That's all right, then.

Rubin You think that's all right? For us both to be paid the same?

Martin Isn't it all right?

Rubin 'Mentoring project'. I'm the bloody mentor.

Wangenroth Mr Rubin, the sponsorship policy of our Foundation . . .

Rubin Never mind, just provide the whisky. Have you a favourite Scotch, Martin?

Martin Should I have?

Rubin Listen, Lowland whiskies are boring, but Highland whiskies are like smoke, like drinking cigarettes. You have to try Speyside malt! The Spey flows through the Eastern Highlands down to Balmoral. Unforgivable to a good Scotsman. But the most balanced whiskies come from that region. Cragganmore may not be the best in the world, but it's very drinkable.

Martin I'll bear it in mind.

Rubin Where was your play performed?

Martin Hanover. In the studio space. It's rather extravagant, I don't think it'll have many productions.

My second play, which is *Without a Title*, the one we're going to be working on, makes more modest demands.

Rubin It doesn't have a title?

Martin Yes, it's *Without a Title*.

Rubin Do you intend to give it a title?

Martin No, it already has one.

Rubin Are you two married?

Martin For two years.

Rubin But you've been together much longer than that.

Martin How do you know?

Gina Five years. We've known one another since we were students.

Rubin History of art?

Gina God, you know that as well?

Rubin I know a bit about people.

Wangenroth I already . . .

Rubin Where's the whisky?

Wangenroth Just a minute.

He goes into the house.

Rubin Naturally, everyone has to find their own way. I can advise you, but if you're any good, you won't listen to me. Anyway, you probably only applied because of the money.

Martin I didn't apply.

Rubin You didn't?

Martin Not that I'm aware of.

Wangenroth arrives back with whisky and glasses.

Rubin He didn't apply?

Martin I was invited, I said yes.

Rubin I thought there was some talk of advertising the opportunity. Wasn't there?

Wangenroth Yes, but . . . finally we decided to approach significant young authors ourselves.

Rubin Why?

Wangenroth Circumstances . . . How shall I put it . . . The applications . . . How shall I put it?

Rubin No one applied.

Wangenroth No, they did.

Rubin But no one you could take seriously.

Wangenroth Well . . .

Rubin You needed a young playwright with a name, but nobody applied even though you were offering ten thousand euros.

Martin It wasn't ten thousand to start with.

Rubin They upped the offer?

Martin Considerably.

Rubin So at first they offered you less?

Martin It's all water under the bridge.

Rubin That means to begin with you turned them down.

Pause. General embarrassment.

The Foundation advertised, but no playwright with any sort of a profile applied. Then you decided to ask a few young authors, including him, but no one would accept. Then you upped the offer, until he finally agreed.

Wangenroth If you put it like that, it creates a quite inaccurate impression.

Rubin Give me a whisky.

Wangenroth hands him a glass. Awkward silence.

Gina People probably felt intimidated.

Rubin What do you mean?

Gina Who's going to dare submit their play to you?

Rubin Yes, I suppose that could be it . . . Did you feel intimidated?

Martin Enormously.

Gina The important thing is, we're all here now. I took an extra week's holiday. To be able to come out to the country. To meet you.

Rubin takes a gulp of whisky.

Rubin This isn't whisky, it's cough mixture. Johnnie Walker! You can really only drink Highland or Speyside malt, even Lowland at a pinch . . . All right, give me your manuscript. I'll read it this evening and we can start in the morning. God willing.

Martin He will be.

Rubin rises to his feet.

Rubin Come with me to my room, please, Mr Wangenroth, you can remove the rug and the television.

He sets off towards the house, then stops in his tracks.

Nobody applied. One day, when you're no longer the voice of your etc., etc., this'll happen to you. Sure as eggs are eggs. People are always asking me why I never wrote another play like *The Long Road*. You know what I say?

Martin Let me think.

Gina Martin!

Martin Maybe you say: 'Who has?'

Rubin glares at him for a few seconds. Then he turns and heads into the house. Wangenroth follows him.

Gina Was that necessary?

Martin Yes, it was necessary. Five days!

Gina It'll soon pass.

Martin Suppose it doesn't? What if it doesn't soon pass?

Gina He was once a great writer.

Martin A century ago. There's a good reason it's been so long since he had a success. All he's interested in is himself, what people think of him and whether they're giving him enough respect.

Gina Perhaps that's how everyone ends up.

Martin Before I end up like that, I'll hang myself.

Gina I don't believe that. Not before, you wouldn't hang yourself before.

Martin Did you just insult me?

Gina I don't think so.

Martin I don't know. I'll have to think about it.

Gina He could do a lot for you. He's still Benjamin Rubin. If he were to recommend you to a big theatre, or write an article about you . . .

Martin Why should he do that?

Gina Perhaps he'll like your play.

Martin Well, I suppose that could happen.

Pause.

Maybe he's not that bad.

Gina You see?

Martin What?

Gina 'All he's interested in is himself and what people think of him.'

Martin Did you really read *The Long Road* three times?

Gina No.

Martin laughs.

Five times.

Martin Have you ever read anything of mine five times?

Gina When no one's watching you, when there's no applause to be had, when just for a moment you're not the centre of attention: that's when you're all the same.

Martin But here, I am the centre of attention. We're here because of me and I'm being well paid.

Gina Can you hear the frogs?

Martin I don't even want to think about how many of them there are. Suppose one of them got into our bedroom . . . !

Gina Is that all nature means to you?

Martin I don't mind nature, as long as it keeps its distance.

He steps forward and concludes his speech.

Ladies and gentlemen, I can't believe he's dead, death doesn't suit him at all. He was the one who taught me that anyone who takes our profession seriously is always a beginner. In this spirit then, as a proud lifelong beginner, I now accept the Benjamin Rubin Award.

Blackout.

TWO

The next morning. Martin Wegner and Erwin Wangenroth are in the garden, waiting.

Wangenroth He has to come down soon. Frankly, I hadn't expected him to be so conscientious.

Martin Is he really reading my play?

Wangenroth He was when I took him his coffee. Spectacles on his nose. Red pencil in his hand.

Martin Red pencil? Red?

Wangenroth Red, yes. Your first play had how many performances?

Martin Twelve.

Wangenroth You do other professional work, do you?

Martin Not at the moment. Thanks to my wife's job at the museum, I don't have to write any more of those dreadful little articles.

Wangenroth I paint. I couldn't make a living from that either. That's why I'm here.

Martin Ah.

Wangenroth I had an exhibition. In Frankfurt.

Martin Oh.

Wangenroth That's Frankfurt-an-der-Oder.

Martin What sort of things do you paint?

Wangenroth Moods.

Pause. Martin looks uneasily at his watch.

Martin Have any of those frogs ever got into the bedrooms?

Wangenroth It has happened, yes.

Martin Shouldn't you instal some sort of grille?

Wangenroth The villa is listed. It belongs to Kurt Freytag, the industrialist, he set up the Foundation. So you can't alter anything. And in any case we're short of money.

Pause. Wangenroth plucks up courage and brings out his iPhone.

This one's called 'Anger'. Acrylic on canvas. And this one is 'Patience'.

Martin Do they sell?

Wangenroth These are still available. If you're interested.

Martin We couldn't afford one.

Wangenroth You don't know what they cost.

Martin And they look too big for our living room. But show them to my wife. She knows more about pictures than I do. Frogs getting into the rooms, has it only happened once, or does it go on all the time?

Wangenroth Actually quite often. Why did you stop writing articles? I write articles as well.

Martin We all do. Everyone who fell in love with books and music and theatre when they were fifteen and thought

17

they were headed for a dazzling future. And ten years later all of us are writing those mean little articles about people who have achieved what we still want to achieve.

Wangenroth But you're not any more?

Martin We had an editorial meeting. We were talking about Kethenwolf's new film, the guy who won an Oscar five years ago. None of us had seen it. We were deciding what to do about it. Somebody suggested an interview, somebody else a profile, and then one of us said: 'Whatever we do, we have to knock this bastard off his pedestal.' And everybody nodded. Took it for granted. I didn't go in the next day or ever again. I was only a stringer anyway. I don't suppose anyone noticed.

Wangenroth Because of one remark at a meeting?

Martin I made the remark. I said: 'We have to knock this bastard off his pedestal.' It was me. I know it sounds stupid, but I was suddenly so disgusted with myself, I simply couldn't go back.

Benjamin Rubin emerges from the house with Martin's manuscript under his arm.

Rubin Morning. So. Now then.

He sits down, lays the manuscript on his lap and starts laboriously going through his pockets until he finds his spectacle case. He takes out his glasses, settles them on his nose, laboriously puts the case away and starts looking for something else. Finally, he produces a red pencil, thinks for a moment, then puts it away again.

Could I have some coffee?

Wangenroth Of course.

Wangenroth goes into the house.

Rubin Sit down, Martin.

Martin does so. Rubin opens the manuscript and leafs through it.

Rubin What kind of font is this?

Martin What kind of font?

Rubin Yes, the font. What kind is it?

Martin I don't know, some standard font. On the computer. Why, is it too small?

Rubin Too small?

Martin I was just thinking. Only because you asked about it.

Rubin Do I look that old?

Martin No! It's just that you asked. . . . Doesn't matter. I haven't a clue what the font is called.

Pause. Rubin leafs through the manuscript.

Rubin Page fifty-seven.

Martin Yes?

Rubin 'It's' with an obviously misplaced apostrophe. I know it's just a typo, but it's better to be aware of these things. Something like that can keep slipping through the net without anybody noticing.

Martin Page fifty-seven?

Rubin Towards the top.

Martin Thank you very much.

Rubin A thing like that: easily overlooked.

Martin Absolutely.

Rubin continues to turn pages.

Rubin After that there are hardly any mistakes. You must have got a new secretary.

Martin I don't have a secretary.

Rubin You mean you type it all out yourself?

Martin I know, it's hard to imagine, isn't it?

Rubin I always had a secretary. But you're right, you can't trust anyone these days, better to do it yourself.

Martin However difficult it may be.

Rubin Well, as I said, later on there are hardly any mistakes. Now, how shall we proceed?

Martin I don't know, I've never done anything like this before.

Rubin Well, be sure to remember the apostrophe on page fifty-seven. Do you want to make a note of it?

Martin I'll remember.

Rubin That's what waiters always say in restaurants, then they forget half your order.

Pause. Finally Rubin makes an effort and begins to read aloud.

'I can see you, but as if from a great distance, like a monster in someone else's dream, like a child's question or the reflection of a mirror in a mirror, like night in a world that has never seen daylight.'

Pause. For a moment it seems as if Rubin wants to say something about this passage, but then he turns more pages.

As I said, in this last third there are hardly any typos.

He puts the manuscript down. Pause.

Where's our tea got to?

Pause.

There's nothing like a big garden! You look around you,
you can breathe more freely, don't you think, and as long
as the weather's reasonable and someone else is doing
the weeding, you can convince yourself that everything's
right with the world. 'Il faut cultiver notre jardin.'
Whereas the house . . .! But what do you expect, the
man manufactures pipelines and that's what it looks like.
It never ceases to amaze, the lack of taste among the
nouveaux-riches! Although taste is only another word for
all those little secret signs we learn early on, designed to
make it difficult for rich pipeline manufacturers to break
into the best society, which there again is the best precisely
because it is so difficult for rich pipeline manufacturers
to penetrate! I remember so well, at the beginning of the
seventies, I was in Italy, writing a screenplay for Fellini,
and suddenly Federico said, quite unexpectedly . . .

Martin It's all right, you can tell me what you don't like.

Rubin I'm sorry?

Martin You don't have to spare me. I'm a grown-up.
Frankly, I'd find it quite strange, if someone like you
didn't find something to object to.

Rubin Someone like me?

Martin Different generations are bound to have different
ideas. But the world keeps on turning. We're never closer
than when we're furthest apart.

Rubin Where'd you get that from?

Wangenroth returns.

Ah, here's our tea.

Wangenroth You said coffee.

Rubin I said tea.

Wangenroth looks to Martin for support, but none is forthcoming. He turns and goes back into the house.

So, how shall we proceed?

Martin At least we're being paid. That's the main thing.

Rubin You're so right . . . We could – I'm speaking theoretically – we could just fake it. We could talk about the weather. Or football.

Martin Yes.

Rubin Are you interested in football?

Martin Not at all.

Rubin Me neither.

Pause.

But we could find something, we could talk about anything for five days, let the time roll by, take our money and go home. No one's in a position to check.

Martin No one.

Rubin But we're not going to make it that easy on ourselves, am I right? Given I've already read it. And I'm sure you'd like to know . . . Am I right?

Martin I am a tiny bit curious.

Rubin Right.

He leafs through the manuscript.

It's just dreadful.

Pause.

Martin Excuse me?

Rubin Dreadful. Completely dreadful. Utterly worthless. Look, it doesn't mean you're not talented. It's just, how can you tell? Not from this. Not when you . . . Not from this.

Pause.

In the last third, there are hardly any typos.

Pause.

I ought not to have been quite so drastic. I'm sorry. I mean, there are passages that . . . .

He leafs through it again.

No, it's all dreadful.

Martin Are you joking?

Rubin If only. I never expected this. Look at this, for example. Picked entirely at random. 'I don't remember who I am. I did know once, or I thought I did, but I've so totally forgotten, I don't even know what it was like to be someone. I envy the dead. They've earned the right to be dead, whereas I've just crept my way in among them, like a child playing hooky.'

Martin Yes?

Rubin Who says that? Who's speaking?

Martin The beginning is about Paul. He died, but now he's back.

Rubin It's Paul's speech?

Martin That's up to the director. I haven't specified.

Rubin He's dead, but he's come back?

Martin I'm not a realist, like you.

Rubin Back from the dead?

23

Martin In a way. Yes. You can take it that way.

Rubin But why?

Martin Why not?

Rubin Because lots of people have tried it. Coming back from the dead. Hardly ever works.

Martin Like I said, you're a realist. I'm not. On stage you're allowed to suggest things and suggesting them makes them true.

Rubin Or take this, for example. 'How come I still have –'

Martin We have very different ideas –

Rubin '– all these questions and all these desires in my heart, as if my dying has not set me free, as if I can still want what I want, without being able to want not to want anything any more?'

Martin – different ideas about what literature is for . . .

Rubin 'As if I can still want what I want.' Sounds good for a moment. But what does it mean? Not to mention: 'Without being able to want not to want anything any more.' If you say it quickly, with a big gesture, it might work for a second. But if you say it slowly . . . 'As if I can still want what I want, without being able to want not to want anything any more.' Let me try it again. 'As if I can still . . .'

Martin Stop! If you read it like that . . .

He imitates Rubin's delivery.

'When Gregor Samsa woke one morning from troubled dreams.' From troubled dreams? What sort of troubled dreams? 'He found he had been transformed in his bed into a monstrous insect.' A monstrous insect? What does

that mean, what are you talking about, what sort of
bloody nonsense is that?

Rubin My dear boy, you must try harder. Do you really
want to . . . ?

Martin No, I don't! I don't want to compare myself with
Kafka, Jesus! All I want to say is: what you just did, you
can do to any text, any text at all!

Rubin Later on there's this second voice, this woman;
I've no idea who she is.

Martin Does everything have to be explained?

Rubin There are no secrets behind sheer crap.

Pause.

Let's start again. I'm sorry. That was unprofessional.
Explain to me. What's it about?

Martin How can I explain it in one sentence? It isn't a
screenplay. If I knew what it was about, I wouldn't have
had to write it.

Rubin You didn't really just say that, did you?

Martin I don't know how to reduce it to a simple plot.
Exposition, conflict, resolution, and then everyone off to
the restaurant and back home. That's the sort of thing
you do, and yes, that's perfectly legitimate, but it's not
what I do. I don't know how we're going to be able to
communicate with one another.

Rubin I don't want to insult you, Martin. As I say,
I imagine you're talented, I'm sure you must be . . . But
tell me . . . I mean . . . Do you absolutely have to be a
writer?

*Wangenroth emerges from the house, carrying a tray
with a teapot and two cups.*

Wangenroth Your tea. Everything all right?

Rubin Just leave us alone.

Wangenroth stiffens, then takes the tray back into the house.

Martin According to you, everything has to be well-organised, provide a clear structure, people need to enter and exit, there must be debates and punchlines and conflict, it's best if the unities of time, place and action are observed, no time-lapses, no ambiguities, and at the end some kind of a surprise twist, but please, nothing too surprising.

Rubin I like experiment. What I don't like is bad plays.

Martin Is it such an unbearable idea for you that times are changing and that there are different approaches and more ways to be a writer than . . . ?

Rubin Yes, there are many ways, but the results can either be good or bad. This is bad. Lifeless and misbegotten. Would-be poetic maundering, but with no poetry, no development, no beginning and no ending. You've written it because at some point you decided to become a writer and you realised no one can be a good writer without actually writing something.

Martin You want me to quote my reviews?

Rubin Yes, I know, you're the voice of your generation. And even this could get good reviews, why not? Any combination is equally probable. Good work gets good reviews, bad work gets bad reviews, good work gets bad reviews and bad work gets good reviews. You know the kind of people who write for the newspapers. Anything can happen. And it doesn't mean a thing.

Martin You have to think that way.

Rubin Why do I have to?

Martin You got your last good review in 1981.

Rubin Even if that was . . .

Martin I'm just saying I'm not the only one who thinks you've lost the plot.

Rubin Which plot?

Martin Many people would say just about every plot.

Rubin And you're one of the people who would say that.

Martin I'm one of the people who say not everything is so cut and dried.

Rubin A lot of things are cut and dried.

Martin Everyone can make a mistake. Even you.

Rubin I can, theoretically.

Martin No question!

Rubin Theoretically.

Martin You could be . . .

Rubin No, I couldn't.

Martin Won't you at least admit that art is always subjective and . . .

Rubin They're not paying me ten thousand euros to admit that art is subjective, they're paying me to tell you what I think.

Martin Perhaps I should try to explain to you what I have in mind with this play.

Rubin You graciously referred to my age. It has its compensations. I don't need things explained to me any more. It's a great blessing. And perhaps it's true, perhaps

27

I did only write one really good play and have been repeating myself ever since. But at least I did write *one* good play.

Martin And I never will?

Rubin Odds are against you. Judging by this.

Pause.

I'm as helpless as you are. We're required to write some sort of joint report about this. That's what they're paying us for. And between ourselves, I need the money. I have rent to pay in three different cities, two very demanding ex-wives and not a sniff of a film deal in years. One classic play, which for the last ten years has only been read in schools and isn't performed any more, is no help at all given my lifestyle; the only thing that can help is film deals. Why do you think I've written all those screenplays? I can't turn down ten thousand. From anyone. But I don't know how I can salvage this.

He stands up.

I'll ask . . . what's his name? I'll ask that young man whether the rules provide for this kind of thing. Something has to be done. And don't take it to heart. I could be wrong. Why not?

He sets off towards the house, then stops in his tracks.

I'm sorry. I'm not wrong.

He goes into the house. Martin sits, motionless. Gina comes out.

Gina I've been watching you. Are you taking a break?

Martin You might say so.

Gina Pretty incredible, seeing you sitting there with Benjamin Rubin. With Benjamin Rubin!

Martin Like something out of a dream, isn't it?

Gina I hope you'll listen to his advice. You can be terribly arrogant sometimes. Think how much experience he has.

Martin He advised me to change professions.

Gina What?

Martin He said I only wrote it because you can't be a writer unless you actually write something. He said nothing about it is salvageable.

Gina Was he joking?

Martin You'd better ask him.

Gina He said that?

   Pause.

I hope you didn't punch him.

Martin You would have noticed. You know I didn't punch him. I should have. I still might. The things he said . . .

Gina Listen to him. Let him explain to you. He wrote one of the –

Martin If you tell me again how much experience he has, I may very well have to kill someone.

Gina He wrote one of the best plays I ever –

Martin Are you trying to tell me he's right?

Gina What?

Martin You keep going on about how great he is.

Gina He's Benjamin Rubin.

Martin And who am I?

Gina What's that supposed to mean?

Martin What do you really think of me? Am I a good writer?

Gina Of course you are.

Martin My last play, *Night, Fog*: you never said much about it.

Gina I said, Stuhlmann's production was very confusing. That chorus! And that actor, what's his name, who kept whispering and rolling his eyes.

Martin Yes, that was bad and there was nothing I could do about it, Stuhlmann told me not to interfere. But I didn't mean that. I meant the play itself!

Gina You know it's not my kind of story.

Martin Not 'your kind of story'?

Gina It was so brutal. So bloody and dark.

Martin And that bothers you!

Gina It's not you. That's what bothers me.

Martin What do you mean it's not me?

Gina It's what you'd like to be. Hard and cynical. How you'd like people to see you. But basically it has nothing to do with you.

Martin And what would have something to do with me? A play about happy bears frolicking through the meadow looking for honey?

Gina Martin, please.

Martin No, explain it to me. What would have something to do with me?

Gina All I said was it wasn't my kind of story. And I'm saying it wasn't really yours either. You'll write different things.

Martin So you didn't like it?

Gina I did.

Martin You thought it was good?

Gina Yes, of course.

Martin Why did you think it was good if it isn't your kind of story? And if it has nothing to do with me?

Gina This is unbearable.

Martin It's a fair question. Benjamin Rubin tells me I'm a failure. And now I'm asking you. In fact, we hardly ever discuss my work.

Gina We hardly ever discuss my work.

Martin Don't change the subject. In your opinion, should I be a writer?

Gina You are a writer.

Martin But should I be?

Gina This is ridiculous.

Martin Is it? My play here, *Without a Title*, I gave it to you a month ago. It's not brutal. It lives by its language. It's a language piece. It's not dark. You gave it back to me and said . . . funny, I can't remember. Did you say anything?

Gina Definitely.

Martin What?

Gina I don't know, it was a month ago!

Martin Then tell me now.

Gina Tell you what?

Martin Did you like it?

Gina Of course.

Martin Why of course?

Gina I liked it!

Martin Really?

Gina Really.

Martin In what way?

Gina Martin, stop!

Martin To be a writer is a decision for life. If someone decides to write novels or non-fiction or plays and he's no good at it, he becomes a ludicrous figure. A laughing stock. Naturally people can make mistakes. Things can go wrong. But if someone's never going to be capable of outstanding work, and if people stop expecting anything from him because everybody knows he's just a failure and he's bitten off more than he can chew . . . Gina, suppose I was someone like that. You'd tell me, wouldn't you?

Gina Of course I'd tell you.

Martin Well?

Pause.

Gina What does 'outstanding' mean, anyway? What one person likes, the other . . .

Martin Don't do this!

Gina It's all relative! Whether something's good or not.

Martin Is that what you'd say to Shakespeare? Or, all right, Benjamin Rubin?

Gina Yes!

Pause.

I think so. Yes, in principle.

Pause.

What about your good reviews?

Martin I asked you. It's very simple. Am I, in your opinion, a good writer?

Gina You could be.

Martin What?

Gina There are very good bits. Sometimes you have . . . a real descriptive talent.

Martin Sometimes?

Gina Yes, that's . . .

Martin Or rarely?

Gina Sometimes! And that's . . .

Martin How often is sometimes?

Gina That's not to be sneezed at! It's more than a lot of people can . . .

Martin And all these years, you've never told me that sometimes I write well and that maybe something could be made of me. Was that your opinion of me?

Gina No, that wasn't my opinion! It is my opinion now because you've asked me, because you're cross-examining me, because you're forcing me to have an opinion.

Martin You mean you don't have an opinion?

Gina You don't always have clear opinions about everything. You don't have to. If you don't get asked, you don't ask yourself. You're not a bad writer, Martin, you could be good, you could be really good, if . . .

Martin But this play? What about this play?

Gina Perhaps something could be made of it.

33

Pause.

Martin We're out of here.

Gina What?

Martin Let's go and pack.

Gina What about the ten thousand euros?

Martin They can keep it.

Gina He's here to give you his opinion, that's what he's done. You can't just . . .

Martin Why are you always on his side?

Gina There are no sides!

Martin Of course not. There are no sides. My mistake. There's only the truth. And that is, he's right and I shouldn't be writing plays. So what's the point of hanging around letting myself be insulted?

Gina You want to run away from him after one single conversation like a . . .

Martin Maybe if I was a better writer or if there was anyone on my side to give me some support. Who was really interested in what I was trying to do. If I wasn't so completely alone.

Pause.

Gina You're completely alone? I'm alone. I earn the money. And when I get home the place is full of dirty dishes, because the great writer can't be arsed to clear the table.

Martin Are you holding that against me? That you earn the money?

Gina The dirty dishes, that's what I'm holding against you. Not the money.

Martin Oh, so this is about the dirty dishes?

Gina We're married, it's always going to be about the dirty dishes. And the hoovering and who takes the rubbish out. And yes, obviously, it's also about the money.

Martin One day. I knew it. I knew one day you'd throw it in my face.

Gina Fine, today's the day.

Wangenroth and Rubin come from the house.

Wangenroth You're having a difference of opinion. I'm hoping I can mediate.

Martin You want to mediate between me and Gina?

Wangenroth No, between . . . between you and Mr Rubin.

Martin What's left to mediate?

Rubin That's what I said. What's left to mediate? Anyway, we didn't have a difference of opinion.

Martin Didn't we?

Rubin Can you define it?

Martin I'm of the opinion I should be a writer, and you're of the opinion I shouldn't.

Rubin I never said that.

Martin Didn't you?

Rubin All right, I did say that.

Martin goes back into the house without speaking.

Wangenroth Mr Wegner, all this can be worked out!

He runs after Martin. Gina and Rubin are left alone.

Rubin This sort of thing only ever works in public. Panel discussions and conversations between painters and writers and composers, all that friendly hypocrisy, all that standing around the breakfast buffet and drinking bad white wine in the evening. All in the pretence that culture is some wonderful Sunday outing for a group of jolly friends. All lies. But he'll get over it. Writers are very hardy. It's just you probably shouldn't marry one.

Gina You should know.

Rubin I certainly should. We only care about ourselves. We justify every piece of bad behaviour by pointing to the great work we're supposedly creating. Of course more often than not what emerges is only a small or medium-sized work. Or nothing at all. And if, once in a while, everything goes right and the result really is a great work, then what? The devoted partner, who's had to put up with all the rages and doubts and worries, discovers she's portrayed in it as the tedious scourge of our daily life. That's what's in store for you, when Martin writes his masterpiece.

Gina You think he's going to write a masterpiece?

Rubin If he's worth anything, he won't let himself be put off by me.

Gina Do you really mean that or are you just saying it to be polite?

Rubin What's wrong with being polite? In any case, I can scarcely imagine my opinion is of any importance to him.

Gina You're not serious.

Rubin Be honest, before you arrived, didn't he make jokes about this? I bet he did. I would've in his position. Jokes about the old fart he'd have to listen to for five days? And at the same time he probably imagined that we'd finish up being best friends. Fantasised that one day he'd win a prize named after me. Already prepared a speech in his head. That's what writers are like. And in all probability you've both been thinking what I might be able to do for him. An article, a recommendation to some theatre . . .

Gina But you wouldn't do that.

Rubin Why not?

Gina You mean you would?

Rubin I have two sons. Neither of them is on speaking terms with me. I've taken every one of my publishers to court and there's an astonishingly long line of women who foam at the mouth whenever my name is mentioned. There's some journalist writing my biography; he wrote to me last week and I just tore up his letter.

Gina Tore up his letter, do people still do things like that?

Rubin All right, I deleted his email. Deleted an email in which he said: 'Many words could be applied to you, but "integrity" is not one of them.' Poor bastard's right. I've always taken the line that I'm an artist and that different standards apply to me. I've never believed that myself. But other people do.

Gina Why are you telling me this?

Rubin Because even with me, corruption has its limits. I can't recommend him to a theatre. I can't do anything for him.

Pause.

I need a proper drink. If they at least had . . . Listen. Highland malts taste like smoke, whereas Lowland malts are usually too bland. But Speyside . . .

37

Gina Cragganmore is the best whisky, but there is no Cragganmore here and I don't want a drink. Thank you very much.

Pause.

Rubin Now I really need a drink.

He starts off towards the house. At the same time, Martin is approaching, carrying a large backpack, a phone in his hand. Since he is staring at the screen – evidently checking the display for the reception signal – the two of them almost collide. For an embarrassing moment, they're in each other's way, until Rubin finally steps aside, passes Martin and goes into the house. Martin dials a number.

Martin Me again, Robert. Yes, it's working now, I came outside, there was no reception indoors. Yes, in the country. How are you? And the children? Great. Fantastic. Very good. I wanted to ask you something. When you agreed to do *Night, Fog* . . . My play. My play was called *Night, Fog*, you directed it! Yes, with Kolpe. Playing the main part. I just wanted to know: what were your reasons? . . . It's difficult to explain. I'll explain another time. Just tell me quickly: why? I know Rebmann recommended the play, but what about you, Robert? . . . In what way is it a stupid question? I mean . . . I mean, did you really think it was good? The play? I'm asking you for an honest . . . What do you mean, raw material? Is a play just raw material? I mean, I know what that means, but . . . All the same, you must know why you . . . Hello? Robert?

He lowers the telephone.

Reception here is a disaster. He said Rebmann gave him the play and he just treated what was on the page as raw material.

Gina What are you doing with your backpack?

Martin Rebmann. The man from the agency. Who's never read my play. Who never reads anything. Who hates the theatre. He was always having us round for barbecues in his garden. It was his recommendation that made it happen!

Gina Put your backpack away.

Martin No, you'd better get your things, the taxi's on its way.

Gina You aren't just going to run away?

Martin You think I should discuss it all with him? Talk until we reach an agreement, until everything's all right again?

Gina Look around you. The trees. Can you even see them? Have you looked at them once since we arrived? Can you smell the grass? Can you hear the crickets? Or the frogs in the pond over there? It's so beautiful here. You and I could simply . . .

Martin Do you remember the way my mother cried at my premiere?

Gina Yes, she was very moved.

Martin I'm not so sure any more.

He taps the display on his phone a few times, then lifts it to his ear. But while it's ringing, something else occurs to him and he lowers his arm.

You wanted a baby. I didn't. Do you remember why not?

Gina Because it would have kept you from your work.

Martin That's right.

Gina Because your plays were more important.

39

Martin Because my plays were more important.

He raises the phone to his ear.

Hello, is this the right number for Mr Magruske? Oh, Mrs Magruske, good morning. It's great to get through to you, I wasn't sure if the landline would still be . . . My name's Wegner. Martin Wegner. We met once a few years ago . . . Could I speak to your husband? . . . What? Oh, my God, Mrs Magruske, I'm so sorry, I'm really . . . My deepest sympathies . . . Yes, we did, very briefly, just for a minute really, but for me it was . . . He wrote about one of my plays, said I was the voice of my . . . May I ask how he . . .? Oh, I see. Ah. Oh, I see. And then he wasn't able to . . . Oh, that's really . . . I'm sorry, Mrs Magruske, let's keep in . . . Goodbye. Goodbye!

He puts the phone away.

What does 'bipolar' mean?

Gina Manic depression. Exhilaration for no reason, followed by profound sadness. Perpetually alternating.

Martin She said no one had been aware of it. One minute he won the Alfred Kerr Prize. The next he . . .

Pause.

Gina What difference does it make? It's still valid. He meant it when he said you were the voice of your generation. Anyway, it doesn't really matter.

Martin It doesn't matter?

Gina What matters is it's not too late to have a baby.

Martin Do you really mean that?

Gina I just said it's not too late. I didn't say I wanted to.

Pause.

You're right. I should have been more honest. To myself and to you. Your first play wasn't great. And this one, *Without a Title*, it isn't great either. I don't know. All I know is, it didn't make me feel delighted or devastated, I didn't even feel happy I'd read it.

Martin Should I destroy it?

Gina Destroy a manuscript. You used to be able to do that. In the same way you used to be able to tear up letters.

Martin I still could. I haven't saved it in the cloud. You know why?

Gina Security concerns?

Martin Yes, can you imagine? I was afraid someone might steal my ideas.

He fetches a computer out of his backpack. He hesitates for a moment and then abruptly hurls it in the direction of the pond.

Gina Martin!

Martin Bullseye. Into the water. Couldn't write, but he had a great aim. And here's the hard copy.

He takes the manuscript, which is still lying on the table and throws it after the computer. Sound of a car horn.

There's the taxi.

Gina You're not leaving!

Martin You can come with me or stay here.

Pause.

I don't think it was because of the work. I think I just didn't want a baby.

41

Gina I don't think I wanted one either. Not yours, anyway.

Pause.

You can do what you like. I'm staying.

The two of them look at one another, then Martin zips up his backpack and leaves. Sounds of a car door slamming and the taxi driving away. Rubin comes out of the house with a bottle of Johnnie Walker and three glasses.

Rubin And you're staying? This is an unexpected development.

He puts the bottle and two of the glasses on the table. He raises the third glass and contemplates it, before putting it down.

Gina He's absolutely beside himself.

Rubin Then you ought to be with him.

Gina I ought to be.

Rubin fills two of the glasses, downs one and refills it.

Rubin Mr Wangenroth is discussing matters with his superiors. Asking what he ought to do, since we're 'in dispute'. That's his phrase. If I don't get my money, I'll sue the arse off him and his Foundation. We could launch a joint lawsuit, your husband and I. Our interests are identical.

Pause.

Did you really read *The Long Road* three times, or did you just want to say something nice?

Gina Did you really think his play was that bad, or did you just want to say something nasty?

Rubin At my age you can afford the luxury of being honest.

Gina Yes, at your age I suppose you can.

Rubin Do you have to do that? Just because I mention my age, doesn't mean you have to as well.

Gina Yes, I'm afraid it does.

Pause. Rubin pushes one of the glasses across to her, she hesitates, takes it and drinks.

In the second act, when Larouche and Oswald meet the con man. It has such a kind of savage melancholy.

Rubin Yes, it's good.

Gina You were only twenty-four.

Rubin Don't remind me.

Gina Why, does it upset you?

Rubin It doesn't upset me that I'm old now. Even when I'm standing in front of a young woman like you, it doesn't upset me as much as it actually ought to. What upsets me is that I've been an old man since then. Since I was twenty-five. Since I wrote *The Long Road* and haven't been able to write anything really great ever since.

Gina Would you like to be twenty-four again?

Rubin Then you'd be too old for me, instead of the other way round.

He refills both glasses. They drink.

Gina You'll see. You've done him an injustice.

Rubin Loving someone means not wanting to see how mediocre they are.

Gina On the contrary. Loving someone means taking their mediocrity on board. Except when you suddenly can't do it any more . . .

Rubin Don't say that.

Gina When Oswald says to the con man that everything is a dream, but we have no idea whose, and when he begs him not to wake him up because he doesn't want it to be all over . . . Is that what you believe? That nothing is real?

Rubin Everything is real. We make the decisions. If you want to, I can be twenty-four again. Anything can happen if we want it to, and if afterwards we wish it hadn't happened, it never did.

Gina But things are as they are. We're either here or we're not. Something's been said or it hasn't been said. You mean something sincerely or you're lying. A piece of work is good or bad.

Rubin Do you really think that? Everything's good and nothing is. Everything's bad and nothing is. How do we know? Who's to decide? Every one of us has told a great many lies thinking we were telling the truth.

Gina That's certainly something you can do: listening to you, it makes me dizzy.

Rubin That's not me, that's the bad whisky. Johnnie Walker. God help us! Don't drink too much of it. It's broad daylight, the birds are singing, as if they wanted to tell us something, but they have nothing to say, except that they exist and we exist, and if we feel like it, the day's already over and it's night, and if we then feel that there's no such thing as night, then it never was night. And I was never too young for you.

Gina That sounds good, but it doesn't make any sense.

Rubin Only if you don't want it to make any sense. You'd have been happy to meet me when I was twenty-four and had just written my play.

Gina The world isn't fair and neither is time. I wasn't born then. And today I'm married.

Rubin Have a drink.

Gina You just advised me not to drink too much whisky.

Rubin So?

Gina Which of us is really drunk?

Rubin Let's assume we both are.

Gina And if afterwards we just decide we weren't . . .

Rubin Then we never were.

Gina And if we like, I could have met you then, before I was born.

Rubin And long before you were married.

Gina And if night should fall . . .

Rubin It's already evening.

Blackout.

THREE

The next morning. Gina and Wangenroth sit at the garden table. Gina is looking at the screen of Wangenroth's telephone.

Wangenroth This one's called 'Anger'.

Gina Interesting.

Wangenroth And this one is 'Patience'. As you see, all in shades of blue and beige.

Gina What about this one?

Wangenroth 'Uncertainty'.

Gina Uncertainty?

Wangenroth Inspired by my work on Heisenberg . Dark blue with specks of ochre. You don't get a very good idea of it on this screen. By the way, I've handed in my notice.

Gina Really?

Wangenroth I had a conversation with your husband yesterday. About how he left his job with the newspaper so he could devote himself entirely to his literary work.

Gina It wasn't a real job. He was just a stringer.

Wangenroth Afterwards, I was very confused. I couldn't sleep all night. I mean, who wants to be an arts bureaucrat? Have you ever asked a child what he wanted to be and he's answered, 'I'd like to organise panel discussions and hand out grants'? It's a profession for the half-hearted, who just want to hover in the vicinity of what they'd really like to do in life. For bystanders and polite hand-shakers, for natural-born fans or people who are totally dead inside. I'm getting out before it's too late.

Gina I hope you've really thought about this.

Wangenroth I see all these artists, week after week, and there's nothing that extraordinary about them, as far as I can see! Most of them are perfectly commonplace, just a bit ruder and more excitable and generally more miserable than your average dentist or weather-forecaster. And they seem to manage it all. They do it, all these people. So I've decided to show some courage.

Rubin comes out of the house.

Rubin Those hideous frogs.

Wangenroth Yes, they were very excitable last night. I couldn't sleep either. Somebody threw paper in the pond.

Rubin Good morning, Gina.

Gina Benjamin.

Rubin Did you book my flight?

Wangenroth For this afternoon. The driver will fetch you in three hours' time.

Rubin That same driver?

Wangenroth I've told him the car mustn't smell of smoke.

Rubin But he mustn't use one of those deodorant sprays! They're utterly toxic. Breathe that in, you get cancer right away. I'd rather have the cigarettes.

Gina I'm taking the train in an hour.

Rubin In any case, we're very pleased we're getting the money after all.

Wangenroth It's not definite. The board has to –

Rubin Let's spare ourselves all those disputes, lawyers, public denunciations –

Wangenroth . . . I'm not authorised to dispense any funds.

Rubin – which won't be much fun for anyone.

Wangenroth We can get this cleared up very quickly.

Rubin I'm sure we can.

　He turns to Gina.

Getting to know you has brought light into my life.

Gina Thank you, Benjamin.

Rubin Maybe we'll see each other again. You never know what fate has in store.

*Martin comes up behind them. His sleeves are soaking
wet and he's covered in mud. He's clutching a few
dozen sodden sheets of paper. The others don't notice
him at first.*

Gina You never know.

Rubin Will you call me?

Gina Maybe.

Rubin I'll be waiting.

Martin Good morning. Everything all right? Enjoying
the fresh air?

Gina Martin!

Martin I got back home and the first thing I did, so as not
to give myself any time to reconsider, was throw the back-
up disk out of the window. It's not as robust as it claims
to be on the packaging and shatters most satisfactorily!
Then I grabbed the last copy of the manuscript out of the
drawer and brought it down to dump in the recycling.
Then I was planning to get drunk as seemed appropriate
after such drastic deeds, but I already felt so drunk with
myself and my decisiveness, it wasn't necessary. I lay
down and slept like a dead man until I woke up with a
start after midnight and wondered if my wife had really
left me and if I'd gone completely insane. So I ran down
to the recycling, but the rubbish men had already been,
since when have they started coming at night? Now I no
longer have a wife or a play, no wife and no play. But
there was plenty of time to think about it before the first
train left, and what do you know, both of them are still
here, the wife and the play, down with the frogs.

Rubin Make some coffee for the young man, Mr
Wangenroth.

Gina You're soaked through.

Martin I got off the train and was happy to find the place really did smell of grass, much as you said, but I'd never noticed, and perhaps that's the way of it, you only smell the grass when you're at the end of the line. So I ran and ran until I arrived at the pond completely out of breath. As I'd thought, there wasn't much left. The ink isn't up to much, it's all washed away, only a few pages in the reeds were still legible. And it took forever to find the laptop in all that mud under the water.

He flourishes the wet, muddy computer.

It's buggered, of course. But there are specialist companies. Perhaps something can be saved.

Rubin That's a load off our minds.

Gina Martin . . .

Martin Listen. Wait a minute. I was down by the water, checking through the pages and I discovered his notes were all over them. In red pencil. – Why did you choose red, Mr Rubin? Who does that sort of thing, who uses red pencil? Accountants? Primary school teachers?

Rubin I realise you haven't a good word to say for me, but I can't allow . . .

Martin Yes, you can, now keep quiet. So what does the red pencil say? Here on page nine, in the margin: 'exc.' E, X, C and a full stop. Might that mean 'excellent'? And here, on page thirty-four, 'exc.' again. See, Gina, am I right? What else could E, X, C and a full stop mean? I can't think of anything. And look, page fourteen, there's a passage underlined: 'As if I can still want what I want, without being able to want not to want anything any more' – and three exclamation marks! Wasn't that the sentence that was so outstandingly bad?

Gina Yes, that could mean 'excellent'.

49

Rubin What are you trying to say?

Gina Does this mean 'excellent'?

Rubin How should I know? I read and I scribble in the margin whatever occurs to me. Afterwards I can't remember what it means. Could be I found certain turns of phrase striking.

Martin Could be you found certain turns of phrase striking?

Rubin It was near the beginning. I was probably desperate to find something good.

Martin Here, page forty-three. Three more exclamation marks.

Rubin An exclamation mark can mean anything. I can't remember. Down here there's a question mark, I don't know what that means either. I always read with a pencil. It's an old habit. Afterwards I never look at it again. When's my car arriving?

Martin Here, on page ninety. That's nearly at the end and you . . .

Rubin For God's sake, leave me in peace!

Martin I'm simply asking: what did you have in mind? Was this part of a plan? Or are you now someone whose incoherent ramblings can no longer be expected to make any sense?

Rubin You'd like that, wouldn't you?

Wangenroth I can't allow this, Mr Wegner.

Martin Oh, yes, you can, if you bear in mind the only alternative is violence. Who's going to stop me? You're weak and he's old. I may be a terrible writer, but I go to the gym. I could knock out a few of his teeth. And the beauty of living in the country is it's hours before the police arrive. You can do what you like. By the time the law shows its face, the whole thing is over. Anyway, don't worry. I'm an educated coward, even when I want to destroy a manuscript I go to the recycling bin. So please, just let me insult him. It costs nothing and it's really enjoyable.

Rubin You find a few pages, you read something into my scribblings, now you're trying to persuade yourself I had some sort of sinister plan. Do whatever makes you feel better. But, tell me – what kind of a plan could I have had?

Martin I have no idea.

Gina I do.

Martin What do you mean?

Gina I believe I have an idea.

Pause. All of them are looking at Gina.

Rubin Gina, think for a minute. How could I have foreseen that he'd run away and leave you here? I'm touched.

Gina You couldn't foresee that, but perhaps you wanted to be as horrible to him as possible and see what came of it. Perhaps that was the extent of your plan, Benjamin.

Martin How come you're on first-name terms?

Rubin And you mean I really thought *Without a Title* was wonderful?

Gina Who knows?

Rubin Right, who knows? Nobody. And nobody will ever know. Doesn't matter what I say, you'll never be certain you're any good. For the rest of your life. Doesn't matter whether you're acclaimed or ridiculed. Something inside you knows that where art is concerned, there is such a thing as absolute judgement. But you'll never discover what it is. No angel is going to reveal it to you. No envoy will arrive from the king. That's what happens to us all. It's like fidelity. No one can ever be sure. We live in uncertainty and we do our best and then we die, and none of it matters in the slightest.

Pause.

Martin What?

Rubin Let's all agree that I'm senile.

Martin Yes, we can agree on that. I'll write better plays. Even if he's right, Gina, he won't stay right.

Gina I'm not sure I care any more.

Rubin Would it help if I say that he's extremely talented? One day people will look back on our meeting, and the fact we met while he was still young will do me great honour. He has a glorious future.

Gina Is that right?

Rubin No one can stop you believing it.

Gina And if we want it to be, it's night.

Rubin And if afterwards we decide it wasn't night, then it will never have been night.

Martin Ah. Now I understand.

Gina Do you?

Martin It's so grotesque, it makes me laugh! She's so much younger than you! Did you really think, just because my wife loves your play, your only play, the only play of yours anyone's ever heard of – did you really think you could persuade us that I'm a bad writer and get off with Gina? Was that it? That's so feeble, so pathetic. So hopeless. This almost makes up for everything, it just fills me with pity.

Rubin As long as it makes you feel better.

Martin I hope you went easy on him, Gina. I feel almost sorry for him.

Gina I did.

Martin I think it makes me able to forgive you.

Rubin That's very big of you.

Martin It must be terrible when your whole life is behind you.

Rubin It's not ideal.

Martin Maybe, when I tell the story later. When I win the Benjamin Rubin Award. Maybe then we'll turn out to have been friends.

Rubin That'd be nice.

Martin extends a hand, Rubin grasps it.

You're not a bad sort. I just wish you were talented.

Martin And I wish you were younger. Then I could knock you down without feeling ashamed.

Rubin Might you need another mentor next year, Mr Wangenroth? I'd be happy to do it for the same fee.

Wangenroth It's not my decision. It'll be someone else's responsibility.

Sound of a car drawing up.

Rubin If I don't get paid for this year, I'll sue the arse off you.

Wangenroth Your taxi's here, Mrs Wegner.

Rubin I'll sue the arse off you!

Gina stretches out her hand, Rubin grasps it briefly, both of them just glance at one another. Then she sets off towards the taxi.

Martin Wait for me!

She doesn't turn round. He runs after her. Wangenroth laughs. For the first time, he looks cheerful and relaxed. Slowly, he brings out a packet of cigarettes, puts one in his mouth and lights it with relish.

Wangenroth Next year, it'll be someone else's responsibility.

He goes into the house, without taking any notice of Rubin. Rubin steps forward. He speaks out front, like Martin at the beginning.

Rubin I don't know what became of my . . . friend Martin Wegner. And I don't care. Soon after that, I woke up one morning to discover that I'd died. Peacefully, in my sleep. Giving up smoking hadn't been much help.

Pause.

Very occasionally, *The Long Road* is revived. Student productions mostly, but I'm not complaining. At any rate, the book's still in print, you can still read it – please do. I don't much want to be a forgotten writer. Resurrections are rare, once you're forgotten, you're generally well and truly forgotten. Sadly the idea of naming a prize after me never occurred to anyone.

Blackout.